THE STORY OF THE
H. L. HUNLEY
and Queenie's Coin

BY FRAN HAWK & ILLUSTRATED BY DAN NANCE

Queenie Bennett gently pressed a gold coin into George Dixon's hand. "Hold this keepsake close to remember my love and bring you good luck," she said.

George Dixon was a handsome gentleman. He looked down at the $20 gold coin and at the woman's face on its surface. Like Queenie, curly hair fell around a face of great beauty.

It was 1862 and George was leaving Mobile, Alabama to fight with the Confederate Army of the South.

George slipped the gold coin into the left pocket of his trousers. Days later, he marched into war as a member of the 21st Alabama Regiment to join the army led by General P.G.T. Beauregard. At the Battle of Shiloh, during some of the most terrible fighting in the war, George felt a sudden sharp burning of a Union bullet in his thigh. He fell to the ground.

George was lucky. Queenie's gold coin had stopped the bullet, saving his leg and his life.

When he returned home to Mobile, George had his precious gold coin inscribed:

Shiloh, April 6, 1862
My Life Preserver
GED

While he would always move with a limp, George would always walk with his lucky coin in his pocket and Queenie Bennett in his heart.

1863
Spring & Summer
Mobile, Alabama

Though his wounds prevented him from returning to the battlefield, George and a group of men planned to build a "fish boat," or submarine, that would sneak underwater to attack enemy ships.

The Union forces blockaded the port of Charleston, South Carolina. The Confederate troops, under General Beauregard, did not have the naval power to break the blockade. Their new fish boat might help open the flow of supplies to Charleston.

Learning and experimenting as they worked, the men molded iron plates into a sleek shape. They added fins, ballast tanks, weights, and gauges. The tube-shaped boat would be forty feet long and four feet deep. There would barely be room for eight or nine men, sitting on a wooden bench, turning the shaft that moved the propeller. Water would be allowed to flow into the tanks and then be forced out to make the craft float or sink in the water.

A long pole was affixed to the front of the submarine. It would hold an explosive, which would be jammed into the hull of an enemy ship. Seconds after attacking, the submarine would make its escape and a line would be pulled to set off the charge.

The most important job fell to the captain, who steered the vessel and operated the levers and pulleys to take in or push out ballast. Inside the submarine, the men would use candles for light.

Horace Hunley

Horace Hunley, a wealthy Southerner who lived in Mobile, helped George and the other men build and pay for the submarine. In honor of his support they called their new submarine the *H.L. Hunley*.

While the *Hunley* was being built, the blockade around Charleston tightened. General Beauregard sent a message to George and the group of men in Mobile. He asked that the *Hunley* be shipped immediately. "It is," he said, "much needed here."

The Confederate soldiers carefully loaded the *Hunley* onto two flatbed railroad cars. They covered the submarine with large swaths of cloth so that it could travel in secret. The *Hunley* was sent to Charleston without George.

George was disappointed to be left behind. "I know the fish boat better than anyone," he told Queenie. "The others don't know how to handle her."

George was right. One disaster followed another in Charleston. The *Hunley* sank the first time when the wake of a passing ship swamped the submarine. Five of the nine crewmen drowned, but the *Hunley* was recovered. Eight new men volunteered, including Horace Hunley, for the second test. When a valve was left open, all seven crew members and the captain, Horace Hunley, drowned.

Back in Mobile, George vowed to take command of the *Hunley*. "I think I can convince General Beauregard to use the fish boat," he told Queenie. Then he reached into the pocket of his pants. "I will take your lucky coin with me," he said. Queenie smiled in agreement.

In Charleston George told General Beauregard, "Sir, the *Hunley* is still in perfect working order. It only sank because the other crews made mistakes. Allow me to choose a crew. I know what I'm doing. The submarine is temperamental, but she is not a death trap. Respectfully, sir, I ask for the chance to try."

General Beauregard remembered George as a brave and determined soldier at Shiloh. Thirteen men had already died trying to navigate the *Hunley*, yet this young soldier was willing to climb down into the submarine to give it another try.

"Go ahead, son," the General said.

George recruited a new crew and made the necessary mechanical adjustments. Finally, on February 17, 1864, the submarine and crew were ready to attack the Union ships in Charleston Harbor.

To operate properly the *Hunley* needed perfect weather conditions. Choppy waters would have made it too hard to navigate. The night of February 17th was cold, but the sea was calm and the moon was bright.

George conferred with the soldiers who would stay on the beach at Sullivan's Island. He reminded them, "When our mission is over, I will flash a blue signal lamp. As soon as you see that blue light, build a big bonfire on the beach. We will follow it home."

That night, before entering the submarine, George took Queenie's coin out of his pocket and rubbed it for good luck.

I will need you tonight, even more than at Shiloh, he thought.

At 7 p.m., George gave the order: "Load up!"

One by one, crew members climbed through the *Hunley*'s front hatch and into its cramped interior. George entered last and closed the hatch. It was dank and cold inside the submarine, but the temperature would rise quickly as the men worked to crank the propeller.

George and his crew hoped to surprise the Union ships moored in Charleston harbor. There was something important that they didn't know.

Two Confederate soldiers had deserted and joined the Union Army. They knew about the *Hunley* and how it worked. Because they expected a sudden attack, the Union soldiers anchored their ships in shallow waters, set up chain nets, and placed big guns on the decks.

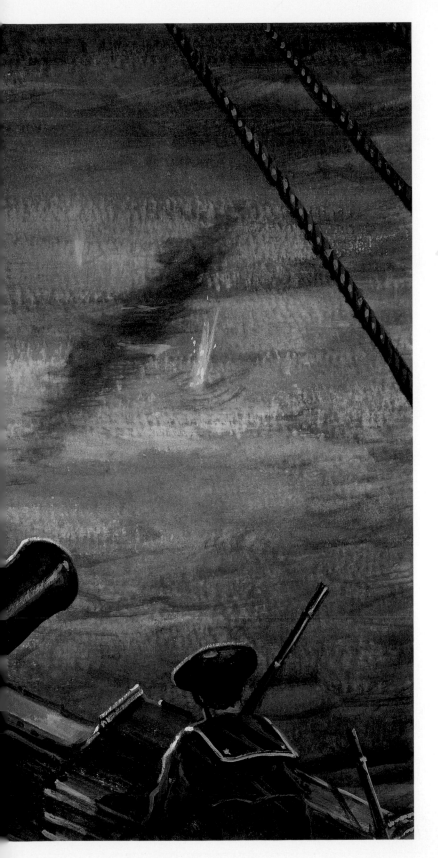

1864 February
Charleston
Harbor

From the deck of the 200-foot-long Union ship, the U.S.S. *Housatonic*, Robert Flemming kept watch that cold, moonlit night. He spotted something floating below. It looked like a huge log.

Flemming shouted out to the other soldiers, who pelted the *Hunley* with rifle fire. But it was too late. A gigantic explosion tore through the *Housatonic*, blasting a huge hole in the side of the ship. Within five minutes the proud *Housatonic* sank to the bottom of Charleston Harbor.

Watching from Sullivan's Island beach, Dixon's comrades were sure they saw the flash of the blue signal light. They followed Dixon's instructions exactly and built a big bonfire on the beach. The men kept feeding the bonfire and waiting. And waiting. They couldn't know that while they kept watch, the candles in the *Hunley* flickered and gave way to darkness.

When the *Hunley* didn't return that night, General Beauregard hoped she had gone to Charleston instead. The next day, however, a telegram relayed grim news. The man who had convinced him to give the *Hunley* one last try was missing along with his seven crew members.

Queenie waited for word of George, but none arrived.

The Confederacy tried to keep the loss of the *Hunley* secret, hoping that the Union would fear more attacks. Any hope of ending the Union blockade ended with the missing submarine and Queenie's George.

As the months passed, Queenie longed to know what happened to George and if her treasured keepsake was still in his pocket.

On April 9, 1865, thirteen months after the *Hunley* went missing, the Civil War ended when Confederate General Robert E. Lee surrendered his troops.

The end of the war was just the beginning of the search for the lost submarine.

The Recovery of the H. L. Hunley

Were the stories about George Dixon and Queenie Bennett true, or had people made them up over the years? Where could the *Hunley* be?

P.T. Barnum, a late nineteenth-century circus owner, offered a reward of $100,000 to anyone who could find the *Hunley* for him to display in his traveling show. Occasionally someone would report a discovery. Each time, further investigation proved the claim a hoax. The sea was busy hiding the *Hunley* and her last crew under blankets of sand. Oceans are very good at keeping secrets.

More than 100 years after the *Hunley* disappeared,

Clive Cussler arrived in Charleston to begin his search for the submarine. He was a Civil War expert, an underwater archaeologist, and an author. "Shipwrecks," he liked to say, "are never where they're supposed to be." Cussler and his team kept looking, on and off, for 15 years.

On May 3, 1995, when the team was exploring a site they had already explored the summer before, a diver found a large metal stump. At first he wondered if it was a boiler from the *Housatonic*. As he felt his way around the object, his hand landed on a hinge. Boilers don't have hinges. Submarine conning towers do have hinges. He wrapped his arms around the hatch and hugged it. He had found the *Hunley*.

All three divers on board the search boat began working to clear the sand from the submarine. Its bow, crusted over with oyster shells and coral, was pointed toward Sullivan's Island. The portside diving plane was in the "up" position, indicating that the *Hunley* had been attempting to surface. Everyone had been looking for the submarine between the wreck site of the *Housatonic* and the shore. Cussler's divers found it on the other side of the *Housatonic* — as though the *Hunley* had been heading out to sea.

August 8, 2000, was a joyful day in Charleston. After five years of planning and fund-raising, the *Hunley* was raised from beneath 3 feet of sand and 27 feet of water from its resting place, four miles off Sullivan's Island. For the first time in 136 years, the *Hunley* broke through the surface of the water into daylight.

The *Hunley* came home to a united nation, healed of its wounds from the Civil War.

A flotilla of boats, from kayaks to yachts, surrounded the site. Hundreds of people cheered and cried. As the submarine passed through Charleston Harbor, Confederate reen-actors fired a 21-gun salute and shone a blue signal light. Crowds of more than 20,000 people gathered around the harbor to greet the submarine.

Senator Glenn McConnell, one of the men most responsible for the rescue plan, spoke emotionally of the *Hunley* crew. "Those fellas," he said, "will not spend another night in the Atlantic Ocean."

Above: *Photo of the H.L. Hunley during 1996 assessment study.* **Opposite page, top:** *Lifting the Hunley out of the water.* **Opposite page, bottom:** *Lowering the Hunley submarine onto the recovery barge.*

The big question of the *Hunley*'s location had been answered.

Now, more questions lay at hand.

Who were the men buried inside her?

How had they died?

Why did the *Hunley* sink?

The *Hunley*'s new home was a coldwater storage tank at the Warren Lasch Conservation Center in North Charleston, South Carolina. A team of experts began cautiously excavating the *Hunley*'s secrets. First, they found the propeller shaft. Then, inside, they found the crew's bench, buttons from the men's clothes, pipes, pocketknives, canteens, a wallet, a brooch, and a corked bottle. These artifacts were exciting, but George Dixon's gold coin was still missing.

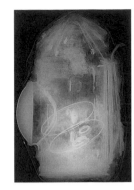

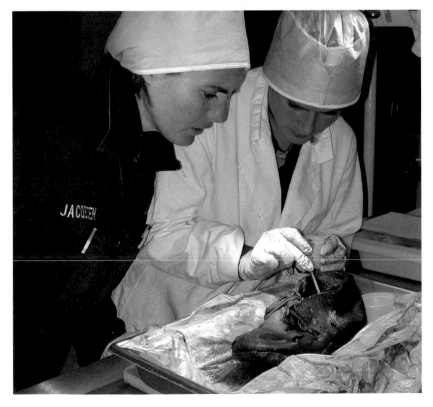

The men had died at their posts. Sadly and respectfully, the workers gathered the remains of crew members for later burial.

The excavation was almost complete. As Maria Jacobsen, the chief archaeologist, carefully explored the mud underneath where Lt. Dixon had sat, she felt something with the tips of her fingers. When the mud was washed away she saw the glint of George Dixon's lucky gold piece. It was almost as shiny as it had been nearly 140 years before, on the day Queenie Bennett gently pressed it into George Dixon's hand.

Opposite page, far left to right: *The reverse side of the Ezra Chamberlin "dog tag." The middle coin is the obverse side of the Ezra Chamberlin "dog tag." Visible bust of George Washington. Lastly, a rubber U.S. Navy button. Over 160 buttons of all kinds were found in the* Hunley. **Opposite page, right:** *The shape of the crank hand positions emerged, indicating the exact stations for the crew. Archaeologist Shea McLean working on the crank handle.* **This page, upper left,** *Conservator Paul Mardikian removing the compass along with conservation intern Ebba Samuelsson.* **Left:** *Archaeologist Maria Jacobsen and Ebba Samuelsson excavating one of the crew's shoes in the lab.* **Above, right:** *An x-ray of the single corroded lantern recovered from the submarine.*

The coin is on display today at the *Hunley* Exhibit at the Warren Lasch Conservation Center.

Horace L. Hunley was honored as a Pioneer of Submarine Warfare when the United States Navy named a submarine tender in his honor in 1962. The U.S. Navy also named a submarine tender for Lt. George Dixon in 1971.

The burial of Lt. George Dixon and his seven crew members was held on April 17, 2004 in Charleston. The funeral was the final one for men who fell in the Civil War. Researchers have not been able to give one specific reason why the *Hunley* sank.

Opposite page: *Archaeologist Maria Jacobsen holds George Dixon's gold coin that she recovered from the* Hunley. **Opposite page, far left:** *A front and back of the gold coin.* **This page, top left:** *Photo believed to be Lt. George E. Dixon, commander of the crew that sank the USS* Housatonic. **Top, right:** *Photo of Horace Lawson Hunley, inventor and builder of the submarine.* **Left:** *Mourners in black period dress attend burial at Magnolia Cemetery, Charleston, S.C. April 17, 2004.*

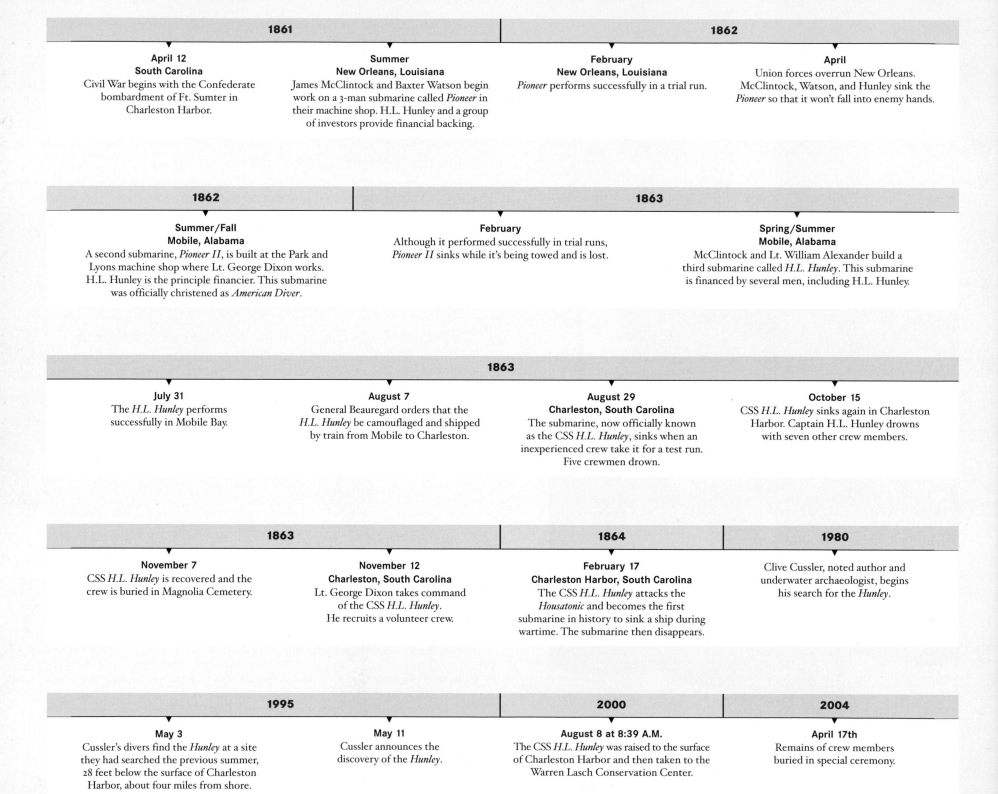

1861

April 12
South Carolina
Civil War begins with the Confederate bombardment of Ft. Sumter in Charleston Harbor.

Summer
New Orleans, Louisiana
James McClintock and Baxter Watson begin work on a 3-man submarine called *Pioneer* in their machine shop. H.L. Hunley and a group of investors provide financial backing.

1862

February
New Orleans, Louisiana
Pioneer performs successfully in a trial run.

April
Union forces overrun New Orleans. McClintock, Watson, and Hunley sink the *Pioneer* so that it won't fall into enemy hands.

1862

Summer/Fall
Mobile, Alabama
A second submarine, *Pioneer II*, is built at the Park and Lyons machine shop where Lt. George Dixon works. H.L. Hunley is the principle financier. This submarine was officially christened as *American Diver*.

February
Although it performed successfully in trial runs, *Pioneer II* sinks while it's being towed and is lost.

1863

Spring/Summer
Mobile, Alabama
McClintock and Lt. William Alexander build a third submarine called *H.L. Hunley*. This submarine is financed by several men, including H.L. Hunley.

1863

July 31
The *H.L. Hunley* performs successfully in Mobile Bay.

August 7
General Beauregard orders that the *H.L. Hunley* be camouflaged and shipped by train from Mobile to Charleston.

August 29
Charleston, South Carolina
The submarine, now officially known as the CSS *H.L. Hunley*, sinks when an inexperienced crew take it for a test run. Five crewmen drown.

October 15
CSS *H.L. Hunley* sinks again in Charleston Harbor. Captain H.L. Hunley drowns with seven other crew members.

1863

November 7
CSS *H.L. Hunley* is recovered and the crew is buried in Magnolia Cemetery.

November 12
Charleston, South Carolina
Lt. George Dixon takes command of the CSS *H.L. Hunley*. He recruits a volunteer crew.

1864

February 17
Charleston Harbor, South Carolina
The CSS *H.L. Hunley* attacks the *Housatonic* and becomes the first submarine in history to sink a ship during wartime. The submarine then disappears.

1980

Clive Cussler, noted author and underwater archaeologist, begins his search for the *Hunley*.

1995

May 3
Cussler's divers find the *Hunley* at a site they had searched the previous summer, 28 feet below the surface of Charleston Harbor, about four miles from shore.

May 11
Cussler announces the discovery of the *Hunley*.

2000

August 8 at 8:39 A.M.
The CSS *H.L. Hunley* was raised to the surface of Charleston Harbor and then taken to the Warren Lasch Conservation Center.

2004

April 17th
Remains of crew members buried in special ceremony.

The Civil War

The Civil War was also called the "War Between the States." Northern states fought against Southern states, brothers fought against brothers. During the four long years of the war, from 1861-1865, more than 600,000 people died.

Southern states wanted to break away, or "secede" from the United States. The South fought for the freedom to run their own economy. The Southern soldiers fought in the Confederate Army. The Northern states wanted a united country. They fought in the Union Army. Both fought bravely with a heartfelt belief that their side was right.

. . . .

The Story of the H.L. Hunley and Queenie's Coin is based on
extensive research in scientific and historical fact
as well as oral tradition. I believe this story is true,
even in the places where no "proof" currently exists.

Sleeping Bear Press
310 North Main Street, Suite 300
Chelsea, MI 48118
www.sleepingbearpress.com

©2004 Thomson Gale, a part of the Thomson Corporation.
Thomson, Star Logo and Sleeping Bear Press are trademarks and
Gale is a registered trademark used herein under license.

Printed and bound in Canada.

10 9 8 7 6 5 4 3 2 1

Library of Congress Cataloging-in-Publication Data

Hawk, Fran.
The story of the H.L. Hunley and Queenie's coin / written by Fran Hawk ; illustrated by Dan Nance.
p. cm.
ISBN 1-58536-218-2
1. H.L. Hunley (Submarine)—Juvenile literature. 2. Dixon, George, d. 1864—Juvenile literature.
3. Marine engineers—Confederate States of America—Biography—Juvenile literature. 4. United States—
History—Civil War, 1861-1865—Naval operations—Submarine—Juvenile literature.
5. Charleston (S.C.)—History—Civil War, 1861-1865—Juvenile literature. 6. Charleston (S.C.)—Antiquities—
Juvenile literature. 7. Gold coins—Anecdotes—Juvenile literature. 8. Underwater archaeology—South
Carolina—Charleston—Juvenile literature. I. Title.
E599.H4H39 2004
973.7'57—dc22

2004009803